The BOY WHO MOVED CHRISTMAS

Words by ERIC WALTERS and NICOLE WELLWOOD
Art by CARLOE LIU

NIMBUS
PUBLISHING
— NIMBUS.CA —

Nimbus Publishing Limited
3660 Strawberry Hill Street, Halifax, NS, B3K 5A9
(902) 455-4286 nimbus.ca

Printed and bound in Canada

NB1447
Cover Design: Heather Bryan
Interior design: Jenn Embree
Editor: Penelope Jackson
Editor for the press: Whitney Moran

Library and Archives Canada Cataloguing in Publication

Title: The boy who moved Christmas / words by Eric Walters and Nicole Wellwood ; art by Carloe Liu.
Names: Walters, Eric, 1957- author. | Wellwood, Nicole, author, writer of afterword. | Liu, Carloe (Illustrator), illustrator.
Identifiers: Canadiana (print) 20200271555 | Canadiana (ebook) 20200271563 | ISBN 9781771089111 (softcover) | ISBN 9781771089128 (EPUB)
Subjects: LCSH: Leversage, Evan, 2008-2015—Juvenile fiction. | LCSH: Christmas stories. | LCSH: Cancer in children—Juvenile fiction.
Classification: LCC PS8595.A598 B69 2020 | DDC jC813/.54—dc23

Canada

Nimbus Publishing acknowledges the financial support for its publishing activities from the Government of Canada, the Canada Council for the Arts, and from the Province of Nova Scotia. We are pleased to work in partnership with the Province of Nova Scotia to develop and promote our creative industries for the benefit of all Nova Scotians.

This story is dedicated to the memory of Evan and the ongoing lives of his brothers, Logan and Tyson.

"It's snowing," Evan said.

"In October," Tyson added.

The two boys, along with their older brother, Logan, sat at the window and looked out. Off to the side a machine was making real snow. The flakes billowed up into the air and settled onto their lawn and drifted down the road.

"It's beautiful," Tyson said. "I never thought it would snow this early."

"Today anything is possible," Logan said.

"Anything?" asked Evan. "I don't know. Santa *never* comes in October."

Logan just winked at Tyson.

In the corner of the room was a beautifully decorated tree with presents underneath. The whole house, inside and out, was decorated for Christmas. Beside the tree were piles of Christmas cards from around the world wishing Evan a Merry Christmas. There were bright lights and a big blow-up snowman smiling and waving on their front lawn. Most of the other houses on their street had lights too.

Two police vans pulled up in front of the house and parked in the snow. Officer Danya and Officer Ken stepped out.

"Mom, they're here, it's time to go!" Tyson shouted excitedly.

Logan offered his hand to Evan. The bump in Evan's head made him unsteady on his feet, but his big brother was always there to help.

Everybody got on their shoes and coats. Evan zipped up his police jacket. Officer Danya and Officer Ken had arranged for him to be made an honorary officer. He had always dreamed of joining the police when he grew up.

Evan, his brothers, his mother, and his best friend, Myles, climbed into the first van with Officer Ken. Other cousins got into the second, driven by Officer Danya.

"Are you ready for your tour?" Officer Ken asked.

The other boys yelled "YES!" and Evan nodded.

"I wonder," he said quietly, "if we'll see anyone...special."

Officer Ken just winked at Logan.

They drove along the street. It really did look like Christmas. Along with the lights, many of the homes had giant signs: "Merry Christmas, Evan!" and "Merry Christmas Evan, Logan, and Tyson!"

Evan liked those best.

"I don't think I've ever seen the neighbourhood so decorated," Officer Ken said.

"Especially in October," Tyson added.

"Never in October."

They went from street to street and then passed the school all the boys attended.

Out front was another huge "Merry Christmas, Evan!" sign!

Next they drove through downtown. It seemed like every store window was filled with Christmas lights and decorations and signs. Two girls were playing carols on their violins and people sang along.

Evan turned his head to get a better look. One of his eyes had stopped working, but what he could see filled his head and his heart. It was all so amazing.

He caught a glimpse of a red coat in the crowd and stared. Could it be?

No, it was a mother holding her baby. Not Santa.

They had to drive slowly now. The usually quiet streets were alive with thousands of friends and strangers.

"I've never seen so many people," Evan said.

"They're all here for you," Officer Ken said.

Evan shook his head. "They're all here to see Santa. I hope they're not disappointed."

"I hope so too. We have to get back now. The parade can't start until the guest of honour is in place."

People now lined their street. On the lawn, the big inflatable snowman seemed to be waving to Evan as he got out of the van and sat with his family in front of their home.

"Is Santa coming now?" Evan asked his mother.

"Soon, very soon," she promised.

"But *how* will he know to come in October?"

"He knows you're celebrating early this year," she said.

"Hmm," replied Evan.

They all sat waiting as big fluffy flakes of snow drifted through the air. Tyson tried to catch them on his tongue.

Down the road they could hear sirens screaming and horns blaring. Red and blue lights flashed as the first four fire trucks of the parade arrived. They all stopped and saluted Evan and his brothers. Evan was also an honorary firefighter.

More sirens followed; an ambulance was next. Through his illness Evan had befriended the paramedics, and they'd made him an honorary paramedic as well. So he was a police officer, a firefighter, and a paramedic! Everyone wanted Evan on their crew.

Next were police vehicles—vans and cars, motorcycles, and even a golf cart and police dogs. Officers walking by wished Evan a Merry Christmas. Evan proudly waved back at his fellow officers.

Then the floats began!

There were antique tractors and cars, big four-wheel-drive trucks, and more trucks towing floats. Everything was decorated with lights and tinsel, trees and presents. Evan beamed as he watched elves and nutcrackers, clowns and angels, and even a Christmas pony parade by.

Dancers, horse-drawn wagons, singers, and a marching band with drums and bagpipes followed. There were bubbles and lollipops, bright lights and music. Float after float, truck after truck, the parade went on and on. And it seemed like every one of them stopped right in front of the family. They waved and called out "Merry Christmas!" or came over to shake hands with the family.

Evan was so happy, he didn't even need Santa to come. He had seen thousands of special people, and he was all filled up with Christmas magic.

But then—

"There he is!" Tyson yelled.

They all looked up the street and saw him...

Santa!

Leading the way were the reindeer rising into the air with Rudolph, his red nose shining, in the front. Mrs. Claus smiled from a bench as Santa soared above a house.

The float got closer and closer and then it stopped right in front of Evan and his family.

"Santa is waiting," Officer Ken said.

"What for?" Evan asked.

"He wants you to join him."

Evan could hardly believe his ears. Officer Ken helped him to his feet and toward the float. As the rest of the family climbed up and sat down beside Mrs. Claus, Officer Ken helped Evan into the sleigh. Evan hesitated at the top.

"It's okay," Officer Ken said.

"Come on up," Santa said as he offered Evan a hand. "I've got you."

Evan took his hand, and with help from Officer Ken, settled in right beside Santa.

"Okay, Rudolph, time to go!" Santa called. The float started again.

From street to street they travelled with Santa. Evan saw people smiling, their eyes sparkling.

"Everyone is so happy to see you, Santa!" said Evan.

Just then, someone called out, "Merry Christmas, Evan!"

Santa looked down at him. "Seems like they're more excited to see you, pal."

Evan's smile got even bigger.

It was Christmas.

Christmas in October. Christmas for Evan.

It had been a long day. Evan was barely able to keep his eyes open as his mother put him to bed that night. She was happy to see him so happy.

As she kissed him goodnight, she bent down and whispered in his ear, "Evan, I'm so glad you could have another Christmas."

"It wasn't just another Christmas," Evan answered. "It was the *best* Christmas!"

A WORD FROM EVAN'S MOM

My name is Nicole Wellwood. I was blessed with three wonderful children: Logan, born on September 17, 2006; Evan, on September 14, 2008; and Tyson came into the world on April 29, 2010. While this story is about Evan, in many ways it is about our whole family and the impact Evan had on us, our town, and on people around the world. Like a stone dropping into a pond, the ripples spread far—but they were strongest at the centre, and the centre is our family.

It all began so simply. I noticed that Evan had a lazy eye, which ran in our family. Doctors weren't concerned until they ran a CT and saw a brain tumour in the worst possible location. We went through denial, upset, anguish, and then did what needed to be done. Treatment began October 2010.

Every Wednesday for seventy-two weeks, Evan received chemotherapy. The hospital became part of his life, but he would dance, laugh, and say hello to everybody when he was there for treatment or blood work. Nurses, doctors, other patients, and the cleaning staff saw not only how brave he was but also how happy. Staff described him as a ray of sunshine. Evan once said to his aunt Ashley, "I stop myself from crying because when I smile everybody else smiles."

Chemo was just part of his routine in some ways, but it also became part of who he was. Evan was a fighter, not a complainer. He always seemed brave and optimistic, and the rest of us drew strength from his positive attitude.

All through junior and senior kindergarten, Evan received regular scans. The tumour—which we called "the bump" in his head—wasn't growing. It was stable.

In September 2014, Evan entered Grade 1. I think he was proud to be a big kid like his older brother. I was proud of him. But everything changed that year.

Evan was having issues moving. There was weakness in his legs and arms. Over the Christmas holidays I noticed more changes that concerned me. I contacted his doctor and another scan was done. It revealed what we had all feared: the tumour had grown. Evan soon began an intense round of chemotherapy and radiation—five days a week for six weeks. This meant long stays in the hospital.

Throughout this time, I read to Evan. We would go to the hospital gift shop and search for new books by his favourite author, Robert Munsch—they always made him smile. While receiving radiation I would read him *Love You Forever*. It was his most favourite book, and it continues to mean so much to me.

Later that year, Evan was so happy to start Grade 2. I was scared for him, but happy too, caught up in his excitement, watching him run and play and spent time with his best friend, Myles.

Three weeks into the school year he woke up with weakness in his legs. He fell walking down the hall, and then again in the kitchen. An emergency scan the next day showed the tumour had grown and branched out.

The doctors told us that there was no further treatment possible. My son, my Evan, was going to die. Nothing that had come before could prepare me for those words.

Evan's doctors had always been supportive and honest with us. They'd explained the chances. But somehow you always think your child will be the one to overcome the odds. Maybe because he'd already overcome so much, I just hoped he'd overcome everything. Evan had always been a fighter and I had learned to be a fighter too. He had always been an optimist and I'd learned to be an optimist. Now there was no fight left and no hope.

They told me his time left could be as short as a few weeks or as long as a few months, but that the end could be marked with significant problems. They told us that if Christmas was important, we should plan to celebrate it much earlier than December 25.

I think the only thing that kept me moving forward during those weeks were my children. They all needed me, and I needed to be strong to help Evan through this last stage of his life.

The counsellors at the hospital suggested

we make a wish list of things Evan wanted to do. His list included eating at his favourite places, seeing *Hotel Transylvania II*, going on the 4D SpongeBob ride, visiting Niagara Falls... and having one more Christmas.

Our family planned to have Christmas on October 19—two weeks after the terminal diagnosis. With that plan in place we went off to spend a weekend at Niagara Falls. But my cousin Shelley had another idea. On October 14, she delivered flyers to our neighbours and to local businesses, requesting they put up Christmas lights and decorations two months early. What followed was unbelievable.

Soon, the entire town of St. George—known as the Friendly Village—became the caring village. Lights were strung up everywhere. Police, paramedic, and fire departments became involved. Evan became an honorary police officer, paramedic, and firefighter. People from far and away decorated for Christmas. And then they decided that for Christmas to come early, Santa Claus and his parade had to come early too. The idea caught on like wildfire. Requests to enter floats in the parade came from everywhere, including the United States. As the number of floats soared to over 250, organizers had to start turning down entries—it could have been bigger than the Macy's Thanksgiving Day Parade in New York City!

On October 24—ten days after the flyer was first sent out—the parade took place. My family, Evan, and his brothers sat on chairs in front of our house. The lawn was covered with snow specially made for the day. Float by float passed as we watched and waved. Then,

as Santa's sleigh passed Evan, the man in red invited Evan up to ride the rest of the parade at his side. Thousands of people lined the parade route. They waved and cheered and called out Evan's name. He waved and smiled. He was happy and he made other people happy.

I'll never forget how a whole town came together to help make a dream come true for one little boy. Throughout the town, across the country, and even internationally, people opened their hearts to make his last wish come true.

Evan peacefully died in my arms at 5:45 a.m. on December 6, 2015, in the Steadman Hospice in Brantford. There was a beautiful smile on his face—despite the fact that for weeks prior he had no ability to move his face. He died in peace.

His nanny, Grandpa Lyle, and his great-grandparents, Nana and Poppa, were at his side. His room was filled with blue and yellow Minions. There was a pin-up board filled with cards from around the world.

Evan always loved reading and being read to. I picture him looking down, reading this book over my shoulder, and laughing and giggling the way he always did.

Although Evan is gone, there are other children, and other families, who continue to go through the same battle. I feel an obligation to help. Those wishing to can make donations to Evan's Legacy, knowing that the funds will go toward helping children and families who are keeping hope alive. Evan would have wanted it that way.

In love and with hope,
Nicole